This Book Belongs to:

....

A NEW BURLINGTON BOOK
The Old Brewery
6 Blundell Street
London N7 9BH

Consultant: Fiona Moss, RE Adviser at RE Today Services
Editor: Cathy Jones
Designer: Chris Fraser

First published in the United States in 2013 by
Part of The Quarto Group
QEB Publishing
6 Orchard, Lake Forest, CA 92630

www.qed-publishing.co.uk

A CIP record for this book is available from the Library of Congress.

ISBN 978 1 60992 578 9

Printed in China

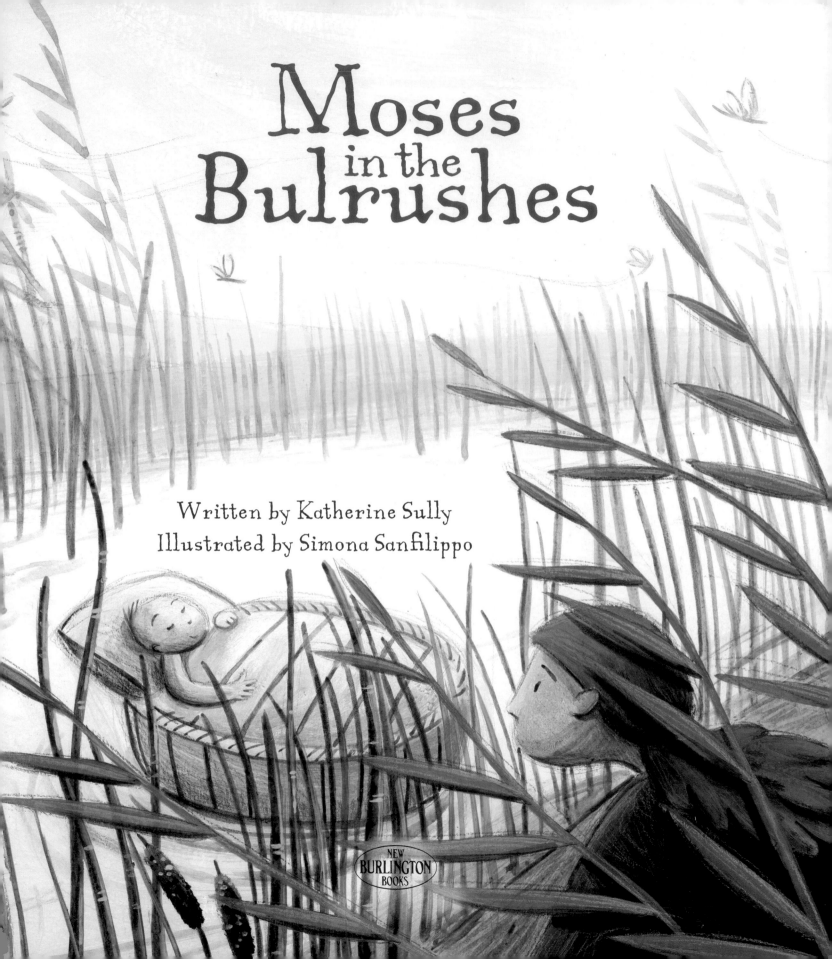

Moses
in the
Bulrushes

Written by Katherine Sully
Illustrated by Simona Sanfilippo

NEW BURLINGTON BOOKS

Once there was a girl called Miriam who lived in Egypt. Her family were Hebrew slaves.

There were many Hebrew slaves in Egypt working for the king.

One day, the king gave an order:
"There are enough Hebrews in Egypt.
There must be no more baby boys."

The king sent soldiers to
all the Hebrew villages.

If they found any baby boys,
they would kill them!

Miriam's mother had a baby boy.
"What are we to do?"
Miriam cried.

Miriam's mother hid the baby in the house and Miriam watched over him.

"Shh, little brother. Be good for Mother!"

But when the baby was three months old, he was too big and too noisy to hide in the house any longer.

Miriam's mother found a basket and painted it so that it would not leak. Then she wrapped the baby in a blanket and put him in the basket.

When no one was looking, Miriam and her mother
carried the basket down to the river and hid it
among the bulrushes.

Miriam's mother hurried back to the house, leaving Miriam to watch the baby. All day, Miriam hid nearby to make sure the baby was safe.

"Shh, little brother. Be good for Mother!"

Then, from her hiding place, Miriam could see some people coming.

The king's daughter was
walking on the riverbank
with her servants.

She saw something floating in the bulrushes.
"Fetch that for me to see," she told
her servant.

The servant brought the little basket to the king's daughter. It floated just like a little boat! The king's daughter looked inside the basket . . . . . . and was amazed.

"It's a baby boy!" she smiled.
The king's daughter lifted
the baby from the basket.

The baby began to cry.

Just then, Miriam jumped up
from her hiding place.

"Shall I fetch someone to feed
the baby and look after him
for you?" she asked.

"Yes, that's a good idea,"
said the king's daughter.

Miriam ran to find her mother, and together they hurried down to the river.

"I will pay you money to feed this baby and look after him for me," said the king's daughter.

And she handed the baby to his mother.

Miriam and her mother were very happy.

They took the baby back home and cared for him until he was old enough to go to the palace.

The king's daughter was delighted. "I will bring him up like a son," she smiled. "I will call him Moses."

Next Steps

Look back through the book to find more to talk about and join in with.

★ Copying actions. Be a little basket bobbing in the bulrushes.

★ Join in with the rhyme. Pause to encourage joining in with "Shh, little brother. Be good for Mother."

★ Counting. Count five birds, five butterflies, three slaves and three vases.

★ Colorful flowers. Name the colors of the flowers by the river, then look back to spot the colors on other pages.

★ All shapes and sizes. Compare the basket and chest that Moses is hidden in as he grows.

★ Listening. When you see the word on the page, point and make the sound— Shh! Wah!

Now that you've read the story…what do you remember?

★ Who was Moses?
★ Why did his mother hide him in a basket?
★ How old was Moses when he was taken to the river?
★ Where did Miriam hide the basket?
★ What happened when the king's daughter came to the river?
★ When did Moses go to live at the palace?

What does the story tell us?
Sometimes our enemies can become our friends.

VOL. 179, NO. 6

JUNE 1991

NATIONAL GEOGRAPHIC

EAST EUROPE'S
DARK DAWN 36

OFFICIAL JOURNAL OF THE NATIONAL GEOGRAPHIC SOCIETY WASHINGTON, D.C.

WILDLIFE AS CANON SEES IT

MANED SLOTH RANGE

Maned Sloth

Genus: *Bradypus*
Species: *torquatus*
Adult size: Length,
  approx. 60 cm;
  tail, 6 cm
Adult weight: 3.5—4.5 kg
Habitat: Atlantic coastal
  forests in eastern Brazil
Surviving number:
  Unknown
Photographed by
  Neil Rettig

The maned sloth moves with slow deliberation through the upper rainforest canopy. But despite its slowness, the sloth is remarkably agile. Hooklike claws anchor its position, while strong limbs and flexible joints afford it great maneuverability in the treetops. Life for the maned sloth is in danger as its forest home rapidly gives way to logging and development. To save endangered species, it is essential to protect their habitats and understand the vital role of each species within the earth's ecosystems. Photography, both as a scientific research tool and as a means of communication, can help promote a greater awareness and understanding of the maned sloth and our entire wildlife heritage.

EOS 1
The New Classic

NATURE

Canon